# Why Stripe A Lighthouse?

by
## John Austin

Printed in the United States of America
Published by
Tryon Publishing Company, Inc.
P.O. Box 1138
Chapel Hill, North Carolina

Cover Design by John Austin
Book Design by Julia Calhoun Williams


ISBN 1-884824-09-9

# DEDICATION

To my proofreader, life's companion, and wife, Emily,
who copes with my phonetic spelling, hit or miss punctuation,
and excesses for strikeovers without complaints.

# ACKNOWLEDGMENTS

With thanks to Senior Chief Jack Downey, commanding officer at the Brant Point Coast Guard Station on Nantucket Island and his second in command, BM1 Gordie McClay XPO, who filled in the gaps of my ignorance with unflagging good humour.

To the following native Nantucketers who were out here at the right time: the late Bob Caldwell, founder and prime-mover of the Nantucket Lifesaving Museum, whose personal memories and voluminous files were like a computer hotline to the national archives; Billie Grieder, son of a career lighthouse keeper, whose memory bank never failed me.

To Maurice Gibbs, born and bred on Nantucket who returned after a Navy career with an encyclopedic memory of early days on lighthouse stations; Byron Coffin, the quintessential New England waterman and his wife, Jennie who, between them, could answer any question that I might ask about anything. To Rennie Stackpole, historian and curator of the Penobscot Marine Museum in Maine, who fed me inside material on Main lighthouses, and whose grandfather was keeper at Sankaty Head for many years. And to anyone else at the Downyflake Coffee Shop, who might have had a question popped at them from time to time.

# TABLE OF CONTENTS

# P R E F A C E

From the first signal bonfire high on a bluff to the automated, high-intensity beams of present day, warning lights have guided water craft away from reefs, around shoals, across great lakes, and into harbors.  The first lighthouse was erected at Boston Harbor in 1716, but it was 1789 before light stations fell under the jurisdiction of one entity -- the United States Treasury Department, headed by Alexander Hamilton.

In 1820, one of the more notorious Department figures, Steven Pleasonton began his penurious 32-year reign.  An archetypal bureaucrat, he stubbornly avoided replacement and had little care for the quality of lighthouse construction or for the keepers' training and safety.  In 1852 the Lighthouse Board was formed.  It established specific guidelines for construction quality and issued elaborate instructions for the keepers which were strictly enforced, resulting in increased pride and morale.  The Board also established awards for bravery as many keepers risked their lives to save victims of shipwrecks.  Over the next fifty-eight years they raised the lighthouse establishment to the most highly regarded in the world.

Eventually the Board organization grew into an unmanagable bureaucracy and in 1910 the Bureau of Lighthouses was established with one commissioner as head, for the first time putting the entire navigational aid system in the hands of civilians.  In 1915 the Life Saving Service was joined with the Revenue Cutter Service to form the Coast Guard, and in 1939 the Bureau of Lighthouses was brought under the Coast Guard, finally consolidating all navigational aids, life-saving, and coastal protection services under one umbrella.

The Lighthouse Board early on began the installation of Fresnel lenses to improve the intensity of the lights.  Electrification began slowly with the first electric light in the Statue of Liberty torch in 1886.  By 1900 the transition to electricity accelerated and was completed in the 1930s.  This new technology resulted in the automation of lighthouses, and the keepers who had loyally tended the old oil lamps were becoming obsolete.  By 1990, they were all gone.

Almost eight hundred lighthouses remain.  Some five hundred are still in use by the Coast Guard.  Of the balance, a number are on the National Register of Historic Places, part of State parks or historic sites.  Many have been turned into museums or are in private hands, and many owe their existence to some determined preservation groups.

It is hard to appreciate the difficulties and hardships endured by those who constructed light stations and those who were the keepers in so many wild and remote locations.  The isolated and exposed sites left keepers and their families at the mercy of ferocious weather -- many were lost.

John Austin's paintings are an important contribution to the record of American Lighthouses.  The monochromatic images communicate clearly -- water's edge, ocean air, rough seas, sand point, rocky ledge, danger, isolation, dignity, time past.  How many of us are here because a small distant light led our ancestors safely home.

# FORWARD

The two airborne Coast Guardsmen on the cover are engaged in painting a broad red stripe on the tower of the 146-year-old Sankaty Head Lighthouse high on the bluff of the eastern shore of Nantucket Island, 20 miles off the coast of Cape Cod, Massachusetts. They are members of a work party from the buoy tender *White Sage*, based at the time in Woods Hole at the western end of Nantucket Sound. Their leader was Chief Warrant Officer George Basset, now retired and living on Nantucket, content and in charge of the commercial boat basin in the harbor.

This was considered rather happy duty, a welcome change of pace from hauling, chipping and painting buoys. They spent a week out in the warm April sunshine, a hundred feet above the deep blue Atlantic, cooking their meals on an improved charcoal grill, made by slicing a 44-gallon oil drum in half, and perhaps doing a little fishing. After they slap on the last brush-full of paint, the tower will look new for about five years.

When a vessel at sea picks up a landfall and the navigator sees that broad red stripe in the middle of the white tower atop a high bluff in the daylight hours, he knows without a doubt that he is off Sankaty Head, Nantucket, and will work his ship accordingly, keeping in mind the various shoals with which he must reckon.

Cruising the U.S. coasts, rivers and Great Lakes, you will see lighthouses with spiral stripes, red, black or brown stripes, diamond-shaped designs, vertical stripes, white towers, red brick towers and square, octagonal and conical towers. Each one will identify itself as a day mark and tell the navigator exactly where he is.

After dark, of course, the characteristic flash sequence of the light will serve that purpose. As we are in an age of technological wizardry, ships equipped with Loran and EPS can plot their position within a few feet so lighthouses have diminished importance but are still useful to small boats and as a check on the sophisticated equipment.

Lighthouses in the last decade of the twentieth century, as dramatic as they appear, have been abandoned by the Coast Guard excepting for the lighting systems which have been retained as aids to navigation. Many minor and remote units have been boarded up and left to the tender mercies of vandals. A few major stations such as Chatham, Cape Cod and Point Judith, Rhode Island have become office space and housing for small boat station crews. Nobska Point on Cape Cod serves as a residence for the group commander.

There are no more manned lighthouses, but many are still lit by the Coast Guard and are automated so that they turn themselves on at dusk and off at daybreak. When a bulb burns out it can replace itself. Some lighthouses rate cosmetic attention from the Coast Guard, especially those on active duty on government property like Chatham Point,

Judith, Rhode Island, and Brant Point, Nantucket, Massachusetts. An abandoned and neglected lighthouse is a target for those insensitive vandals who are titillated by the sound of breaking windows and who are addicted to aerosol artwork.

Many others have been "adopted" by local historical groups who have the energy to restore and care for them. There have been some inspiring rescue projects, such as that at Sakonnet Point, a little "coffee pot" tower on a pile of rocks, a mile or so off Little Compton, Rhode Island. It rusted away for several years, the cormorants flying in and out of the empty windows until a particularly energetic group of light house buffs undertook to rehabilitate it, operating by small boat out of a nearby ship yard. Another equally dedicated band of zealots undertook to give the same treatment to the Rose Island Light, under the Newport Bridge at Newport, Rhode Island and the Sakonnet Point Light across the bay.

Some retired lighthouses have been purchased by private individuals for a seaside cottage such as has been done by Jamie Wyeth, the son of Andrew. In any case, it will be a long time before they disappear from the scene.

This book is not an encyclopedia of New England lighthouses -- better writers than I have already done that. I am merely dipping into my personal memory bank and relating a few spontaneous anecdotes that come to mind. My map indicates a "bunch-up" of stations in the immediate vicinity of Long Island and Cape Cod. That works out because I lived in Connecticut for over twenty years and spent a year on Long Island during World War II plotting German submarine movements and networking with the Coast Guard who were staffing the nation's lighthouses at the time.

The lighthouse establishment was run by civilians until 1939 when the Bureau of Lighthouses was brought under the direction of the Coast Guard which then assumed the duty. The change-over was benevolent; the keepers, usually older with families, were allowed to hang on until retirement or, if younger, enlist in the "Guard."

In my rambles over the years, I have encountered several of those civilian keepers and have "picked their brains" about lighthouse keeping. In recent years I have discovered that a coffee shop buddy was the son of a keeper who did hitches at Great Point on Nantucket and Gay Head on Martha's Vineyard, and he has been able to fill in gaps in my knowledge. Just last summer, I met a fellow at a Coast Guard Chief Petty Officer's gathering who had spent twenty-one years in the service on the Maine Coast. His colorful recollections were invaluable.

One of my treasured possessions is a dog-eared copy of *Laws, Rules of the Lighthouse Establishment of the United States*, dated 1852. After a few pages of officialeeze, and "be it enacted" admonitions, it starts right off with the meat of the matter: "The lamps shall be lighted at sunset and extinguished at sunrise." What could be simpler?

Actually there was more. A great deal could happen from the time the keeper shrugged into the primitive storm clothes of the time, left his warm, cozy quarters, and scurried across the open ground through a gale-force northeast blizzard to the light tower. As the steel door clanged shut, he climbed up the drafty spiral stairs (sometimes a hundred or more) to the lantern room where he performed his four-hour stint. All of the oil lamps must be lit and the wicks trimmed several times a night. The reflectors needed constant attention with a polishing rag as did the glass chimneys as they smoked up.

Life was a tad easier for the keeper if blessed with a fixed light because the clockwork apparatus of a flashing or occulting light had to be periodically re-wound. The heavy counterweight dropped all the way to the ground level within the thick pipe that the spiral stairs wrapped around. The instructions sternly cautioned that any downtime on this mechanism could alter the flash characteristic of the light and cause a shipwreck.

During particularly bad weather when the window glass was obscured by snow or ice, the beleaguered keeper had to again don his storm gear and go out on the gallery walk-around to scrape for an hour or so.

In milder weather, if fog threatened, down to the outbuilding which contained the horn machinery and fire up the ear-splitting diaphone or siren. Several days of this could ruin a sensitive keeper's equanimity. Back in the 'good old days', the fog warning system consisted of a canon discharged at regular intervals. There was no time for 'snoozing' in the tower, as the keeper was expected to keep a record of shipping passing by the station and log the time and a description of each vessel. In the event of a shipwreck, he had, if possible, to interview the survivors to determine if or when any saw the light.

During the off-watch time there were plenty of housekeeping chores to occupy the keepers. Presumably, in family stations there were one or more women on the scene, including female siblings, to do the work on the distaff side, but there were still plenty of other duties: house-painting, carpentry, yard work, bookkeeping, controlling the inventory of stores, and, if on an island, insuring that they didn't run out of beans, potatoes or flour before the supply boat arrived. Those are just a few of the duties that a keeper was obliged to perform for his four hundred dollars per annum.

The era of lighthouse operations is for the most part on the wane, but they are such romantic and wonderful structures as they perch on the high bluffs and rise up more than a hundred feet out of the narrow beach sand dunes. I find it difficult to put my admiration into words.

*John Austin*
*March 1996, Nantucket*

# Why Stripe A Lighthouse?

# ❀ CONOVER RANGE LIGHT ❀
## LEONARDO, NEW JERSEY

By golly, it's still there! After all these years, I thought it might have been replaced with a shop by now.

As a small boy, enjoying my second summer at the shore, I played in the sand near the Conover Range Light, making constructions out of driftwood and shells, and paddling in the warm shallow pool that appeared at low tide just for my pleasure. I must have been under adult supervision but it was never intrusive. There was a lady named "Mom" who shared my house, a tacky little summer cottage with exposed studs. I slept in an upstairs bedroom that was redolent of cedar and mothballs. A dormer window displayed a crystal wind chime that tinkled in the salt-flavored breeze that ruffled the white curtains. There was also a pleasant man who smelled of shaving lotion who only appeared on weekends. He was known as "Dad."

I was the only pre-schooler on the block, but being born with the ability to amuse myself, I had a good life: swinging on the fence gate and enjoying the sights, sounds and smells of the summer hotel on the other side of the fence. There were the clicking of croquet balls, the thunking of tennis balls, evening band concerts, the laughter of the guests and the jangle of silverware at meal times.

This was the golden era before power lawn mowers, boom boxes and noisy mopeds; the occasional whirring of a hand-pushed mower was the loudest intrusion on our tranquility.

The modestly-scaled lighthouse resembled a 20-foot pipe standing on end and was painted white with a red band around the middle. It was a friendly sight as it blinked out its flash at night. I was modestly-scaled myself and the tower seemed to go right out of sight into the sky.

I was happy to see a story that appeared recently in *Lighthouse Digest* about the restoration of Conover Range by a dedicated band of local lighthouse buffs.

---

*1855*

# ❀ NAVESINK LIGHT ❀
## HIGHLANDS, NEW JERSEY

During the summer of my tenth birthday, my family rented a basic little cottage overlooking Sandy Hook Bay in the Atlantic Highlands. Actually, it was right on the border of Waterwhich, a seaside village noted for party boats, lobstering, clamming and thirty-two bars. We were situated on a wooded bluff with a set of plank steps leading down to the railroad tracks of the New Jersey Central at the water's edge.

In those days, a little steam-powered commuter train met the New York boat to distribute its passengers along the coast until it ran out of track in the posh town of Bay Head, twenty-five miles away. The benevolent conductors would make stops anywhere for the convenience of the passengers.

I slept in an attic bedroom with a dormer window facing South which exposed me to a 25-million candlepower flash from the Navesink lighthouse, the first to be equipped with the Fresnel lens. It sits atop a high headland a couple of miles down the coast. A heavy black curtain saved my sanity but rendered the room a little stuffy on hot nights.

One sunny day in August, my good buddy of the summer, a peer member named Dick, and I packed peanut butter sandwiches and Oreos and hiked down the oyster shell road to Highway 36, where we spiraled up the access road to the lighthouse. Architecturally unique, Navesink resembles a Romanesque fortress, composed of twin sandstone towers connected by a crenulated service building containing the keeper's quarters. A civilian keeper and his family were in residence. The keeper took us upward into the south tower to show us the spectacular view of the entire coast which stretched all the way to the Manhattan skyline. From this vantage point we could see the constant parade of ships traversing the Ambrose Channel.

In 1949 the light was automated and reduced in candlepower. In the mid '50s the old Speraceti Lifesaving Station, with its artifacts, was brought up from Sandy Hook and a state-sponsored museum dedicated to the history of lighthouses and of the U.S. Life Saving Service was established.

*1828, 1862*

# ❋ Sandy Hook Lighthouse ❋
## Sandy Hook, New Jersey

The white octagonal masonry tower of the Sandy Hook Lighthouse has been one of the most successful construction projects since the Pyramids. It came in under budget and has performed without flaw for 232 years, making it the oldest surviving lighthouse in America. At the present it looks good for another century or so. The only sour note would be the realization that 200 years of reverse erosion has put it in a pine forest a considerable distance from the ocean. In other words, it no longer enjoys the status of prime waterfront property.

For several years it shared space with Fort Hancock, whose battery of enormous disappearing coastal artillery guns protected New York City and its New Jersey neighbors from hostile invasion. To date, they haven't been asked to fire in defense.

For a brief time prior to Pearl Harbor, I was dating the young daughter of the commanding officer and had easy access to the base, if one could consider twenty miles on a bike easy access.

As the Coast Guard had taken over the Lighthouse Service two years before there was considerable pressure to switch the keepers over and there was a certain amount of resistance. Of course, some of the older "Wickies" (a nickname taken from the large wicks used in the oil burning lamps of early lighthouses) were past the Coast Guard age limit for entry so they were permitted to serve out their time until retirement.

---

*1764*

# ❁ Beavertail Lighthouse ❁
## Conanicut Island, Rhode Island

I first saw Beavertail from the water, while traversing the East Passage of Naragansett Bay, headed for Newport Harbor. It was winter, and snow covered the ground. The square granite tower and the white stucco keeper's house were a dramatic composition atop the rocky bluff, surrounded by a rip rap breakwater. It was being bombarded by ten foot waves and the spray was high in the air. The fog diaphone was "bloooing" mournfully and the lantern on the tower was flashing a green light eight times a minute as it guarded both entrances to the Bay. It was an experience that will remain in my memory.

I made a second visit a couple of years later by a land approach, armed with a camera. The Coast Guard keepers had departed to other duties but still maintained the optics for navigational needs. The buildings have been adopted by the Rhode Island Parks Association for the summer tourist trade.

Beavertail has taken quite a few "hits" from hostile foreigners over the years since its construction in 1749. That date makes it the fourth oldest lighthouse in the nation. During the Revolutionary War, the "Brits" used it for target practice and at the conclusion of hostilities, burned it down in a fit of pique.

In 1815, the keeper's dwelling collapsed into the water and history does not relate whether the keepers were still in it at the time. This disaster had been expected because it was too close to the sea and made of inferior materials. In 1848, the inspectors pointed critical fingers at the tower, and it was replaced in 1856 with a square granite tower. I am happy to say it has survived to this day, automated, electrified and beloved by local lighthouse buffs.

_____

*1749, 1753, 1856*

# ❀ BRANT POINT HARBOR LIGHT ❀
## NANTUCKET

Because it is within biking distance of my house, I spend a lot of time walking the beach around the Brant Point Light. Nantucket weather runs the gamut at Brant Point: sunrise, sunset, rainy, snowy, foggy, cloudy, partially cloudy, red sunrise, red sunset, yellow-tinted sunrise, light snow, deep snow, light breeze, full gale, hurricane. I have seen it all and have made paintings of every nuance of weather, time of day, and season.

It is a much photographed location; professional picture-takers flock here for views suitable for calendars and magazine illustrations, not to mention post cards. In the summer, tourists come to swim, take the sun, hold wedding parties and wave good-bye to departing house guests as the car ferry rounds the lighthouse on the way to the mainland.

The woeful history of this light is filled with disaster -- destruction by fire and storm. The diminutive structure was re-built eight times over a 150-year span.

The Coast Guard small boat station on the property holds the key to the lighthouse and hangs a king-sized wreath on it at Christmas, but the actual servicing is done routinely by the Aids to Navigation team in Woods Hole, 40 miles up the sound to the west. It is, of course, only a harbor light and its little red flash is seen for just a few miles at sea. On foggy days, of which Nantucket has more than its fair share, I can hear the synchronized horns, one at the lighthouse, the other out on the end of the East Breakwater, sounding ten seconds later.

---

*1746, 1759, 1774, 1783, 1786, 1788, 1825, 1856, 1901*
*(1856 structure also survives)*

# ✹ PEMAQUID POINT LIGHTHOUSE ✹
## PEMQUID POINT, MAINE

I have personally visited the Maine lighthouses that can be reached by land, and Pemaquid is by far my favorite. My choice is based on the charm of the keeper's quarters and the view of the ocean. I can visualize myself sitting on the porch in the summer, watching the marine traffic going in and out of Miscongus Bay to Newcastle or Damariscotta.

Pemaquid was built in 1827 to guide shipping into the bay. The first keeper, Isaac Dunham, was obliged to raise his own vegetables because he had so much arable soil on the property; this was an unusual circumstance because many of the off-shore keepers had to carry soil out in baskets and pray that the brisk Maine sea breezes would not blow it away.

Isaac had the reputation for being a tad slippery which was borne out when he built several out buildings on the property at his own expense and then attempted to extract rent from the next keeper after his transfer to another station.

There were shipwrecks aplenty at this location, the best known being the fishing vessel *George F. Edmunds*, which attempted a short cut to the mouth of the bay in 1903 and ran hard aground due to a navigational miscalculation. There were only two survivors.

---

*1827*

# ❋ BARNEGAT LIGHTHOUSE ❋
## BARNEGAT INLET, NEW JERSEY

The original lighthouse at Barnegat Inlet, halfway between Sandy Hook and Cape May, New Jersey, was constructed in 1835. The designer was a retired ship's master named Winslow Lewis.

Lewis was the developer of a superior optic system involving an argand lamp and parabolic mirrors but he was a little shaky on lighthouse construction. The tower, at forty-five feet, was too low to be seen an adequate distance at sea and showed serious deterioration problems after twenty years. However, his engineering shortcomings were overlooked by his good friend, Stephen Pleasonton, head of the Lighthouse Service.

In 1855, an astute and experienced inspector recommended a taller tower made with stronger materials. So in 1858, the present structure was completed and has since functioned well. To distinguish it from the other tall towers on the Jersey coast, the upper half was painted a tasteful burgundy.

Serious erosion problems threatened in the 1930s and it looked like doomsday for old "Barney." In the interest of historical sentiment and tourism, a fund-raising campaign was mounted country-wide, even asking school children whose contributions, as modest as a quarter, were welcome. Enough was collected to construct two rip-rap breakwaters and the noble old lighthouse still stands.

Barnegat Inlet is just about the trickiest on the Atlantic Seaboard and any boater who wings it on the wrong tide is in for a stressful experience. I ran it many years ago at the helm of a thirty-eight foot Richards inboard and lost control, scraping one of the black and white mid-channel buoys.

*1835, 1858*

# ❊ GAY HEAD LIGHTHOUSE ❊
## (FROM THE WATER)
### MARTHA'S VINEYARD, MASSACHUSETTS

I did a painting of Gay Head Light shown on page 70 because I wanted to include the original keeper's quarters which have since been removed, leaving only the tower. The reference for that piece of work was a photo loaned to me by the son of one of the keepers in the 1930s. Recently, I had an opportunity to take a photo from a small boat just below the colorful clay banks from which Gay Head derives its name and include that view here.

Of historical interest at this location is the notorious wreck of the *City of Columbus* that occurred on the Devils Bridge Ledge during the winter of 1894. This disaster happened when the coastal steamer wandered off course during a zero-visibility snowstorm and ran up on the ledge, resulting in over a hundred fatalities. The keeper, a Wampanoag Indian, was the hero of the night as he rounded up a crew of fellow tribesmen to launch a boat to effect a rescue mission, making several hazardous sorties out to the wreck for survivors. The last two off the wreck were unfortunately frozen in the rigging and had to be cut loose to be brought ashore.

*1799, 1856*

# ❈ EXECUTION ROCKS ❈
## SANDS POINT, NEW YORK

There is a pile of rocks, placed by Mother Nature, at the western end of Long Island Sound where it joins with the East River. Thirty feet of water flowed over it at low tide, but clearance for a large vessel was a little too marginal, so more rocks were added in 1850 and a charming little lighthouse was constructed.

Since there was no dwelling for the keeper, he was obliged to row out from the shore. As this routine was a little tedious, a rugged granite house was built in 1867. This was a building that millionaires on the upper East Side of Manhattan would be happy with.

There was precious little exercise space on the concrete platform, but a little cautious power walking could be done around the perimeter. For a more vigorous workout, one could go up and down the spiral stairs of the tower. On a nice summer day, the keeper could bring a canvas chair out and watch the ships go by. A keeper wanting to combine his pleasures could take the station skiff over to New Rochelle for a taste of urban life.

The macabre name is derived from a grisly period during the Revolution when Yankee patriots were caught harassing the British. The climate of hostility was such that the death penalty was usually invoked. Not wanting to grant these prisoners an opportunity for public martyrdom, a plan was devised to let the tide take care of it out on the rocks in the Sound.

The Lighthouse Board made provisions for superstitious keepers who might be squeamish about living in proximity to the famous drowning pit. They were given the opportunity to transfer so they wouldn't be nervous about the subterranean "ghosties."

---

*1850*

# ❦ GREAT POINT LIGHT ❦
## NANTUCKET, MASSACHUSETTS

One morning in March, 1985, just before dawn, in the aftermath of a wilder than usual Northeast storm, the pilot of a commuter flight radioed the Nantucket control tower to report that the Great Point Lighthouse was dark. This was reported to the Coast Guard and the repair team that responded discovered a shocking fact: the problem was not merely a burned out bulb; the entire lighthouse had washed out to sea, leaving only a few bricks, a couple of twisted stair treads and the battered roof of the lantern.

The Coast Guard quickly erected a substitute facility, built of 4-by-4 timbers with a light on top and a checkered orange and white sign for a day mark. This would have served mariners well into the next century but for the tears shed by the historical buffs who wrote copious letters to their legislators. At least one letter found its way to the desk and attention of Senator Edward Kennedy, who pulled a string or two for funds to rebuild the lighthouse.

Such clout is not unusual on Nantucket island. In the mid 1970s, the Coast Guard changed the antique Fresnel optic system on the Sankaty Head Light for a modern aircraft-type revolving beacon, removing the traditional lantern housing on top of the service room. The resulting naked appearance generated so much wrath among purists that a letter from one fetched up in the Oval Office, and the Coast Guard was "asked politely" to replicate the original.

The Great Point job was completed in 1987, with a full-fledged dedication, complete with dignitaries, fireworks and speeches. A fleet of private boats and Coast Guard vessels were set to swarm out to Great Point on the appointed evening, but alas, a dense fog rolled in and the event was delayed for twenty-four hours.

---

*1784, 1818, 1987*

# ❋ Farallon Islands ❋
## San Francisco

During the San Francisco gold rush, a steady stream of sailing vessels flowed in and out of the busy port. Many of them were obliged to pass near the infamous Farallon Islands in an area that was known for heavy fog. It was not unusual for a vessel unequipped with modern electronic gadgetry to run aground on the rocks, inflicting a heavy toll on men and ships.

It was obvious that a lighthouse was needed on the highest peak of the Southeast Island.

Just off-loading material on the island was a major feat of seamanship to be attempted only when the weather was calm. Once ashore, every piece of wood and every brick had to be carried on the backs of the workers, about five bricks at a time. After the station was open, a mule was used to bring supplies to the top.

There is little written about the hardships of those rugged men who spent months out on those jagged rocks in the fog and gale force winds. When one contemplates all the scenic and comfortable locations for lighthouse keeping, an assignment to the Farallons must have been a dismal prospect indeed. It is now automated and, outside an occasional maintenance crew visit by helicopter, only the seabirds inhabit the rock.

*1855*

34

# ❀ ROBBINS REEF LIGHTHOUSE ❀
## STATEN ISLAND, NY

Robbins Reef Lighthouse is a little "coffee pot" shaped facility sitting on a pile of rocks less than a mile from the ferry slip at St. George, Staten Island. It can be viewed from a boat approaching the terminal, although very few passengers ever give it a glance.

I had the opportunity to do a painting commission of it several years ago for a Sandy Hook harbor pilot. He was sentimental about it as he used it for a reference while guiding ships into Newark Bay or Kill van Kull. At that stage of my career, I hadn't discovered the camera as a reference tool and resorted to sketches. I was obliged to make several round trips in order to get the details that I needed. It was a good painting and the pilot was pleased.

A Sandy Hook pilot is a guide who spends half his adult life learning the features of a harbor so he can go to a prescribed location in the Ambrose Channel in a small vessel, meet incoming ships, board them, and instruct the helmsman to take course changes that will enable the ship to reach an anchorage at the outer harbor without running aground. Had the Exxon Valdeze in Alaska had this kind of help a lot of wildlife might have been spared.

The history of Robbins Reef Light parallels that of Kate Walker who raised two children in the little tower while tending the light from 1886 to 1919 after her husband died.

John Walker was keeper at Sandy Hook when he first met Kate, a young German immigrant who had been a waitress in an eatery where John took his meals. There was good chemistry between them and when he was transferred to Robbins Reef, he married Kate and took her along. In a shameless act of nepotism, he appointed her as assistant keeper at an annual wage of three hundred fifty dollars. She nearly fled back to the "fatherland" when she discovered that her little home was entirely surrounded by water. Eventually the cozy environment grew on her and she stayed for thirty-three years.

After John Walker succumbed to pneumonia, Kate was appointed regular keeper and just to keep it in the family, appointed her son Jacob, as assistant. Her daughter, Mamie, boarded on shore during the school year but returned to the lighthouse in the summer.

Kate was a busy lady with a rowboat; in addition to mainland forays, she is reputed to have rescued over fifty individuals who came to grief on the rocks. She retired in 1919 at the age of seventy-eight and took a house with Jacob and his wife.

---

*1838, 1883*

# RACE ROCK
## FISHERS ISLAND, NEW YORK

Sometimes, writing about lighthouses can be a creative challenge as many of them enjoyed a fairly tame history and I am fortunate to find excitement in their background.

Race Rock, a half mile off Fishers Island in Long Island Sound, could keep a platoon of marine writers typing away indefinitely. In John Floherty's *Sentries of the Sea*, he devotes an entire chapter, fourteen pages, to the construction of the stone base that can be seen in the illustration.

The construction difficulties can be summarized with the realization that a fine engineer and a highly experienced marine construction foreman were on the job for over seven years just to build a stable base for the lighthouse. Once the base was completed, the lighthouse was built in less than a year.

In the easy-going 1990s it would be difficult to recruit a labor force who would work for a dollar a day and spend twelve hours up to their necks in cold water, chipping away at granite rocks without benefit of power tools, rubber gloves, wet suits, hard hats or safety goggles.

---

*1856, 1879*

# ✸ HIGHLAND LIGHT ✸
## TRURO, CAPE COD

Highland Light, also known as "Cape Cod Light," was the first lighthouse on the Cape. It was built in 1798 because its presence was absolutely essential for the benefit of vessels coming to Massachusetts Bay from the old world. It was the first indication of the landfall. Its first order light source measured four million candlepower but was replaced by an aircraft-type beacon in 1927 as its importance to navigation waned. The two keeper's houses are now used as quarters for Coast Guard personnel. The light is currently automated.

So much for textbook information. The fact of the matter is that the light is an endangered species, the clay bluff is eating up the lawn at an alarming rate but not without the notice of the Truro Historical Association. What to do? Raise money - lots of money! Get advice - lots of advice. They are doing just that.

In the spring of 1991, the association invited an engineering firm in New York to come and have a look. An engineer spent three days on the Cape where he was wined, dined and housed like royalty. He was so grateful that he produced a usable set of numbers for relocation and the group is now fund raising.

_____

*1798, 1833, 1857*

# ❖ SAYBROOK BREAKWATER LIGHT ❖
## SAYBROOK, CONNECTICUT

Saybrook Breakwater Light is so named because it is on the end of the Saybrook breakwater, located a quarter-mile from the Lynde Point Lighthouse at the entrance to the Connecticut River on Long Island Sound. Check your map, if confused. I have passed close to the light several times while passing between the two jetties on the way out to the sound in a thirty-eight-foot yawl.

The little white tower is a dramatic sight as I coast by with a 10-knot over the water speed. It has obviously been abandoned: its windows are boarded up, rust runs down the sides from gallery brackets and it is marked by droppings from the black cormorants perched on the roof and railings. The light is automated and flashes its light list code.

In the 1960s, when the light was still active, a Coast Guardsman from Lynde Point came out in a Boston Whaler to service the light and attend to maintenance problems.

One summer, ten years later, I drove to Saybrook with the intention of walking out on the breakwater to take a close-up photo to be used for a painting. The Lynde Point Light is out at the end of a prestigious enclave for the super rich called Fenwick, a summer playground for the Governor and assorted CEOs, not to mention a legislator or two.

When I approached the security guard at the entrance, I was denied admission on the grounds that I resembled a tourist. The fellow turned a deaf official ear to my entreaties, but we did strike a compromise. If I showed up after Labor Day, he wouldn't be there. I had to be content with a photo taken from the sailboat ten years before.

---

*1886*

# ❀ Montauk Point Lighthouse ❀
## Long Island, New York

I first met Montauk Light during the winter of 1941-42 as a member of the Army Air Corps and newly organized anti-submarine command on Long Island. At the time, German undersea wolf packs were attacking allied shipping off the coasts of New Jersey and Long Island at an alarming rate. I was assigned to a direction-finding unit on the bluff at Montauk Point.

There was a string of these units about every ten miles along the coast all the way to Cape May, New Jersey. My apparatus consisted of a little plywood box just large enough to accommodate two normal-sized bodies and the instrumentation capable of picking up a radio signal from an offshore submarine chatting with its mother ship at night. This contraption was mounted on a ten-foot pole that permitted a three hundred sixty-degree pivot. Access was via a ladder and an outward-opening door. If one was careless in exposing the door to the infamous Montauk gales, one would spin around wildly until a companion could come to one's rescue.

If we were successful in getting a decent signal, we would phone the plotting section at the home base located in a commandeered summer hotel about a hundred miles down the road to the east. If we were able to get a triangulation fix from three different direction finders, the Navy would dispatch patrol bombers to deal harshly with the U-boats. This sounds simplistic but we were not very good at it in the early stages and some of our fixes were plotted miles inland.

There were three of us in the crew and we were berthed at the Lighthouse. There are happy memories of card games on the kitchen table with the resident "Coasties." But all good things come to an end and I was moved out to another job in New York City.

---

*1797*

# ❋ MONOMOY ISLAND LIGHT ❋

## MONOMOY ISLAND, CAPE COD

Developers salivate when they contemplate Monomoy Island, a barren ten-mile strip of dunes just south of Chatham, Cape Cod, separated by a narrow fast-moving channel. In their dreams, they visualize acres of chic little cottages, a condo or two and a market for t-shirts, all connected by a winding scallop shell road.

Fortunately, the Monomoy National Wildlife Refuge beat them to it in 1977. It is administered by the Fish and Wildlife Service, an energetic group who have made great strides in renovating the buildings in the light-house station.

I visited the Island several years ago when the local Audubon Society ran a boat over for nature walks. I took photos of the lighthouse at the time for painting reference. Due to reverse erosion, the station, once at the edge of the dunes, is now a half-mile inland.

The light itself hasn't officially been on a light list since 1923, when one of the twin towers at Chatham was transplanted to Nauset during the famous lighthouse shuffle.

_____

*1823, 1855, 1870s*

46

# ❉ FERRYLAND LIGHTHOUSE ❉
## NEWFOUNDLAND, CANADA

There will be no poetic here of the Ferryland Lighthouse on the bleak Eastern Atlantic coast of Newfoundland on the Canadian Maritimes. The light tower is a stumpy little reddish brown truncated cone, streaked with rust and gull droppings. Because it is situated on a high bluff, it lacks the stately grandeur of the tall, thin coastal towers on the water level barrier beaches in the United States.

The keepers house is a basic white clapboard structure, badly in need of paint. In its present condition, it resembles the rental houses seen in the more unattractive industrial cities in this country and Canada. Because of recent automation, there is no longer a need for human habitation so, perhaps, the neglect can be forgiven.

At one time several years ago, a family with children lived at Ferryland and the house must have been painted a sparkling white with an orange-red roof for visibility against the winter snow. Windows were washed regularly and the lady of the house most likely planted a little garden during the short growing season for a mix of therapy and fresh vegetables. With solid insulation, triple storm windows, a first class heating system and a connecting shelter to the lighthouse, it must have been a neat and cozy shelter in the winter when the raging north Atlantic gales hammered the house and rattled the windows.

---

*1871*

48

# ❄ LATIMER REEF LIGHT ❄
## FALL RIVER, MASSACHUSETTS

Frank Joe Raymond, a sixteen-year-old living in Bridgeport, Connecticut, had no interest in the normal teen pursuits of his peers. His goal in life was steady employment. Youthful games were not for him. He had been working at the entry level jobs available to boys in 1923 when he heard about an opening for an assistant keeper on the Latimer Reef Lighthouse two miles off-shore from Stonington.

Not one to dawdle, Frank caught a three a.m. milk train up the coast to Stonington and persuaded a local lobsterman to take him out to the lighthouse. Frank was one of those "Horatio Alger Jr." kids who inspire confidence among adults and the keeper liked "the cut of his jib," especially as the boy added two years to his age. The keeper wrote a note for Frank to carry to the lighthouse guard at the New Haven post office, singing high praises of this applicant. There was a shortage of able-bodied young men willing to live and work in a cast iron cylinder sixteen feet in diameter on a pile of rocks two miles off shore. Frank was a shoo-in for the job.

During his eleven years on the reef, Frank was nudged into learning to paint marine scenes, using found canvas and house paints. He developed a fair degree of skill and visits to museums in nearby cities whetted his appetite for an art career. He saved up enough money for two years at the Rhode Island School of Design but lacked the academic credits for admission. Rejected but not daunted, he promptly switched careers. After a battery-powered radio was donated to the lighthouse, Frank took an interest in music and diverted his art nest egg to the purchase of a saxophone which he learned to play well enough to do weekend gigs in jazz clubs in the area.

During the remainder of his lighthouse career, Frank became addicted to physical fitness, working out with weights and rope jumping. He became a rowing aficionado, taking the station skiff the thirty miles round trip to Montauk to have a cup of coffee with the keeper. At least once he sculled seven hours one way to Block Island. However, the Coast Guard insisted upon bringing him home in their motor lifeboat for his own safety.

*1804, 1884*

# BORDEN FLATS ❀ ❀

## FALL RIVER, MASSACHUSETTS

A motorist driving east on US Route 195 over the Braga Bridge at Fall River, Massachusetts can look down at the East Branch of Narragansett Bay and see a little "spark plug" lighthouse a short distance from the bridge.

Painted a sparkling white, Bordon Flats is perched on a rugged granite block base, which is just about big enough for an exercise-starved keeper to do a few laps once in a while. If that wasn't enough, he could take the station skiff over to town for a snack, a beer or a movie.

One of the perks for a Bordens Flats keeper was the proximity to urban civilization. He may have lived ashore and rowed out to service the light. In the winter when weather or ice conditions blocked access, the fellow could be stranded out there for several days. The one unbreakable rule, however, was to never, never be stranded on shore, leaving the light unattended.

There was one instance several years ago at the Romer Shoals Light, a mile off Coney Island, when an assistant keeper was caught ashore by the weather. He attempted to row but the wind and tide were against him, so he caught a ride on a tugboat and jumped overboard when he was close enough to swim to Bordon Flats after bundling his clothes in a waterproof bag.

---

*1881*

# ❀ SAKONNET LIGHT ❀
## LITTLE COMPTON, RHODE ISLAND

I drive to Newport, Rhode Island a couple of times a year on business. In the spring of 1992, while en route via Route 6 out of New Bedford, I made a wrong turn at Tiverton and fetched up in Little Compton on the ocean front. As an artist always ready for new inspirations, I was rewarded with a fishing village, a boat yard, a "closed for the season" eatery, a splendid view of Portugal and the East Coast of Africa and, as a special bonus, a quaint little offshore lighthouse. According to my map, I was standing on the beach at Sakonnet Point just one peninsula away from Newport.

After taking photos, I back tracked a mile or so to a doughnut shop that was not closed for the season where I was filled in on the doings out at the lighthouse. It was still active but automated by the Coast Guard and unoccupied. An indefatigable group of lighthouse buffs who travelled back and forth by boat had put it in mint condition.

When I got home, I checked in my "lighthouse bible" but could only find one small paragraph about it: an anecdote about two keepers in the 1940s who were involved in an intense personality clash. When two people are working in an eighteen-foot diameter cast iron cylinder, compatability is a vital ingredient. But these two fellows cooked and ate separately and went for days without a spoken word. It all came to a bubbling head one day when one pushed the other out the door and locked it. The outcast keeper spent two days in the elements until a passing fishing boat came by and rescued him.

---

*1884*

# ✸ EAST QUODDY HEAD LIGHT ✸
## CAMPOBELLO ISLAND - NEW BRUNSWICK - CANADA

Most inhabitants of the upper Maine seacoast and the summer visitors who flock there each year are familiar with the small red and white banded lighthouse called West Quoddy. It is a calendar and post card publishers dream and as a tourist attraction, Lubec, Maine considers it "money in the bank."

However, one seldom hears of EAST Quoddy Head Light. It guards the northern coast of Campobello Island in New Brunswick, Canada, familiar stomping grounds of the Franklin Roosevelt clan in days gone by. The white octagonal tower emblazoned with the large red cross holds the high ground of a rocky promontory.

The tower keeper's quarters are all interconnected so as to spare the personnel the rigors of a Canadian seacoast winter, where the wind chill is in single digits most of the time.

My painting was done from an old photograph but most likely presents the same aspect today. It is difficult to imagine the keepers and their families playing croquet on a summer's eve on the lawn.

The red cross serves to dramatize the tower against the snow, while the tower is painted white to make it stand out against the dark green pine trees in the background.

_____

*1867*

# ❊ CAPE HATTERAS LIGHTHOUSE ❊
## BUXTON, NORTH CAROLINA

In the summer of 1965, we loaded two progeny, a large shaggy dog, camping equipment and two adults in a 1948 wooden-bodied station wagon and headed for Cape Hatteras, North Carolina. Guarding Diamond Shoals on the "Graveyard of the Atlantic", the tallest lighthouse in America was once considered the most important light on the East Coast.

To shorten a long story, I'll begin with our arrival at the National campground at Salvo, North Carolina on the grand Banks. After selecting a camp site, we set up our two tents and strolled down the road a hundred yards to "downtown Salvo," a mini post office, a mini general store and about ten mini houses on pilings. Having read about the famous Midgett family of lifesaving and Coast Guard heroes on the Cape, I asked the store keeper if there were any Midgetts in the area. He replied, "I be a Midgett." As it turned out, most of the population carried that name.

Prominent in the store parking lot was an antique fire pumper, covered with a tarp. The volunteers, most of whom were Midgetts, held public fish fries every weekend in the summer to raise money to build a proper fire station to get the 1938 American LaFrance out of the weather as it was the only fire protection in the region.

I wandered out in the field behind the store and discovered a graveyard, badly overgrown, about half the size of a tennis court. Many graves were marked with epitaphs indicating that the occupants were unnamed victims of a shipwreck. Leaning against the fence were six stone grave markers, still in their crates, delivered by UPS from Elizabeth City on the mainland. The oldest bill of lading was dated ten years before. Outer Bankers are a laid back lot.

*1803, 1854 (raised to 150'), 1870*

# ❂ FIRE ISLAND LIGHT ❂
## LONG ISLAND, NEW YORK

Fire Island is a super place about halfway out on the south shore of Long Island. It is accessible by ferry from Bayshore and when a visitor disembarks he will not find any taxis, private cars or tour buses. The only vehicles permitted there are the police department jeep and a four-wheel drive fire pumper. Walking is the mode of travel and the occupants of the little cottages haul their groceries and luggage in children's or handsawn wagons over a network of wooden boardwalks.

The Fire Island Light's tall, tapered black and white structure towers dramatically over the dunes and can be seen half way to Europe as a day mark.

During the middle of the last century, this was regarded as the most important light on the East Coast for transatlantic steamers making for New York. It was deactivated in 1973 and still shows an automated light. As Fire Island is a haven for a large number of wealthy New Yorkers, the local preservation society had no trouble raising a million dollars for restoration and other expenses. The plans include converting the keepers dwelling into a museum.

_____

*1826, 1858*

# ❁ ORIENT POINT ❁
## LONG ISLAND

This diminutive caisson-type lighthouse, known as "The Coffee," for obvious reasons, marks the Western end of Plum Gut, a white water channel that connects Long Island Sound with Gardners Bay. I have traveled the length of this channel a couple of times and truly agree that it can be compared to one of those western rivers that provide such adrenaline-filled thrills to "white water" rafters.

The tower is planted on a little pile of rocks a short distance off shore. At the turn of the century, a transplanted Norwegian named Knute Anderson was the first keeper and under the rules at the time was not allowed to share the quarters with Mrs. Anderson who boarded in town for the twenty-year hitch served by her husband.

Weather and season permitting, the lady was regularly visited at her boarding house by her spouse. These visits were frequently cancelled by severe winter icing conditions.

However, Anderson was not totally alone out there. His assistant, Daniel McDermott, an Irish immigrant, turned out to be an agreeable "bunkee" and was able to dispel the cabin fever. I can picture this compatible pair sitting at the galley stove playing cards while the winter winds rattled the windows and shook the tower. They might have even induced a little stimulant into the coffee to ward off the chill.

_____

*1899*

# ❀ LITTLE GULL ISLAND ❀
## LONG ISLAND SOUND

Sailing out of Gardiner's Bay near Orient Point at the Eastern end of Long Island's North Fork, we passed through the "Race," a particularly lively section of turbulent water which can whiten the hair of the most daring mariner. In due course, the wild water abated and we hove into view of Little Gull Island -- bleak, forlorn and abandoned.

The gray granite tower and the keepers house perch on a massive stone base, sixty feet in diameter and eight feet high. The doors and windows are boarded up and the keening sea birds have left their mark on everything. There is little vandalism for it is not easily reached by yahoo boaters.

It is difficult to believe that keepers actually lived out here and performed their duties on these bleak two acres without television or reading material.

In 1854, the records show that an assistant keeper became disenchanted and resigned after a few months on duty. His wages of twenty-five dollars per month might have been a factor. His name was Jubael Poque and his replacement only lasted three months -- an indication that this was not a "dream" job. However, Jubael apparently had second thoughts and returned to the Island a year later. The light was abandoned in 1950 and automated in 1978. There is nothing there now but ghosts and birds.

*1806, 1869*

# ❋ NAUSET BEACH LIGHT ❋

## EASTHAM, CAPE COD

In 1923 there was a great lighthouse shuffle on Cape Cod. Eastham, ten miles up the road to the north, had three undistinguished little shingled structures known as "The Three Sisters." The intention of this arrangement was to make identity a bit easier from seaward. In truth, it only made it more confusing to the mariner.

In time, the lighthouse management agreed and the movers and shakers began to move and shake; the three small towers at Eastham (Nauset) were removed and rented out as cottages in a slick little entrepreneurial maneuver and one of the Chatham towers was unbolted, disassembled and carted up the road to Nauset. After assembly, a red stripe was painted around the top third of the lighthouse to distinguish it from the remaining Chatham light.

_1877_

# ❀ SANKATY HEAD LIGHT ❀
## NANTUCKET ISLAND

Sankaty Head Light is a dramatically sited structure and easily accessed by visitors although it is locked and abandoned. Its magnificent beam, through automation, still sweeps the sky. It can be seen from the car ferry at a considerable distance out in the sound and also from my front yard.

Unhappily, Sankaty is on borrowed time. Under death threat from bluff erosion, there is speculation that it will not last out the year. An ad hoc group was formed in the winter of 1991 in an effort to save the tower from toppling into the sea, as Great Point did in 1985. Brave words were spoken, computers computed, fax machines faxed, ad hoc officers were elected and thousands of man and women hours were expended but the bottom line was the intrinsic cost of moving the structure. Fund raising not withstanding, seven hundred fifty thousand dollars

was an unrealistic goal. The rich folk on the bluff have hired an engineer and there appears to be feverish activity on the beach below the houses. There is a flicker of hope that something can be done to save the houses and at the same time put off doomsday for the lighthouse.

In the early 1980s, Coast Guard families were quartered in the keepers houses which have since been removed. Human nature being what it is, the wife of one family and the husband in the other were involved in just a tad more than a neighborly relationship. When it escalated into a screaming, hair-pulling match in front of a bus-load of tourists, transfers were made to opposite ends of the district.

---

*1890*

# ❀ CAPE FLORIDA LIGHT ❀

## KEY BISCAYNE, FLORIDA

Many lighthouse keepers had moments of reflection when they wondered if this was an ideal line of work: climbing spiral steps up into one hundred fifty-foot towers several times a night to tend the light, living with ear-splitting fog horns for days on end, dealing with winter storms on wave-washed off-shore islands and many other minor irritations that can befall lighthouse keepers. But no keeper in history ever had such a thoroughly rotten afternoon as did two assistant keepers at Cape Florida Light on Key Biscayne on July 23, 1836.

This was at the end of the Seminole Indian wars and lighthouses in remote locations were fair game for marauding bands of Indians. Cape Florida was particularly vulnerable and at this time the head keeper elected to take his family to Key West for their safety. He left his assistant, John Thompson, in charge with an elderly black helper, known only as Henry, for moral support.

On that fateful day, Thompson and Henry were out on the boardwalk when they heard the whooping and yelling that always accompanied an Indian raid. They barely made it to the door of the lighthouse tower. The heavy wooden door was secured with an iron bar, but the attackers were armed with muzzle-loading muskets and wasted no time in putting a barrage through the door.

They missed the human targets but a few of the balls went into the whale oil butts in the area, causing little streams of the contents to arch out and saturate the two hapless keepers as they retreated up the spiral stairway to the lantern deck, closing the trapdoor behind them.

The invaders battered down the entrance door and swarmed up the stairs, inflicting considerable intimidation on the victims above. Thompson held a trump card. He lit the fuse on a keg of powder and dropped it down the trap door. This strategy removed the Indians but also removed the stairway. In the meantime, Henry was killed by an errant musket ball and Thompson's oil-soaked clothes ignited from the flashback of the powder-keg explosion, so he was obliged to remove them. The Indians had scurried off but Thompson was left stark naked out in the hot Florida sun with a ninety-foot drop to the ground and no neighbors for five miles.

In due course, a Navy gunboat, having heard the explosion, appeared on the scene. Getting Thompson to the ground was an exercise in frustration but finally, a messenger line was shot up to him via a musket ball and Thompson was lowered in an improvised bos'ns chair.

---

*1825, 1855*

70

# GAY HEAD LIGHTHOUSE
## MARTHA'S VINEYARD, MASSACHUSETTS

In truth, I have never visited the Gay Head Light even though I have been on the Vineyard. It is not an easy jog from the north end of the island where my business has taken me.

When I was living in Connecticut, I was given a commission to do a painting of it through a local art gallery. In lieu of working on the site, an option that would not be cost effective, I opted for a photo from a travel brochure for reference. The client was happy with the result, but there was one anxious moment about the body of land in the background. Before I could make a wrong guess, the lady suggested "Cutty Hunk of the Elizabeth Islands." I promptly verified that. I have since painted Gay Head many times and I have since learned that the keeper's house has been torn down.

When I moved to Nantucket twenty years ago, I developed a coffee shop counter relationship with a fellow named Billy who revealed that his dad had been the keeper at Great Point on Nantucket in the 1930s and had subsequently been transferred to Gay Head when Billy was in high school. When I showed him my travel brochure photo, he pointed out his bedroom window on the second floor and the basement entry roof that he used for clandestine exiting. Billy told about the negatives of lighthouse living; access to schools was difficult. On Nantucket it had involved a thirty-mile round trip in a Model A Ford with oversized tires. While living at Gay Head on the Vineyard, he went to the Indian school.

_1799, 1856_

# CURRITUCK BEACH LIGHTHOUSE
## COROLLA NORTH CAROLINA

If you like sand, surf and lonely beaches, you'd love Currituck Lighthouse, a tall, slim orange brick spire rising from the dunes on a low lying barrier beach on the Outer Banks of North Carolina. It is about halfway between Cape Henry, Virginia and Bodie Island, North Carolina on State Road 12, and is strategically important to southbound shipping that edges a little close to land in order to avoid the northbound Gulf Stream. It displays a first order white light that can be seen nineteen miles out to sea. The brick tower is one of few that was left unpainted.

The lighthouse has been sitting on a wood timber plumb to this day. There is a dearth of folksy historical lore at Currituck, but it must have been a good berth for a keeper in spite of the 200 man-killing steps that had to be scaled several times each shift.

There is one salty piece of history in the vicinity regarding the abandoned Currituck Lifesaving Station that has been baking in the sun among the dunes since the 1870s. With a little imagination, one can conjure up an image of a crew turning out for a rescue in their black foul-weather gear, hauling a surf boat or a beach cart. There would be flickering flares and much shouting. Hopefully, at the end of the rescue, the surviving mariners would be brought back to the station and bedded down with strong stimulants.

---

*1875*

# ✹ The Eddystone Light ✹
## England

British lighthouse builders made three attempts with the famous Eddystone Light before they got it right. The first, erected in 1696, was designed and contracted by a Henry Winston Stanley who was a total novice in this type of construction.

In all fairness, it was an engineering miracle that he was able to put up even a rudimentary structure. The finished product resembled a country estate standing on end - complete with Jacobean half-timbering, open balconies, leaded glass windows and many other architectural features not ordinarily seen on off-shore lighthouses. He estimated that a sixty-foot height would be more than adequate to clear the oceans, but alas, the first September storm crashed over the lantern top and doused the over-sized candles. Back to the drawing board.

Undaunted, Henry added another forty feet the following spring and specified bigger candles and that seemed to do the trick until the winter of 1703 when the candles, the lighthouse and the workmen were lost in a vicious storm. Back to the drawing board again. A new and improved structure was completed in 1706 with the principal material being granite.

Eddystone number three was built by a proper engineer who knew what an off-shore lighthouse should look like. This one lasted a hundred years; by then lighthouse builders had got the the hang of it and built a new one 150 feet high that has lasted until the present time.

---

*1696*

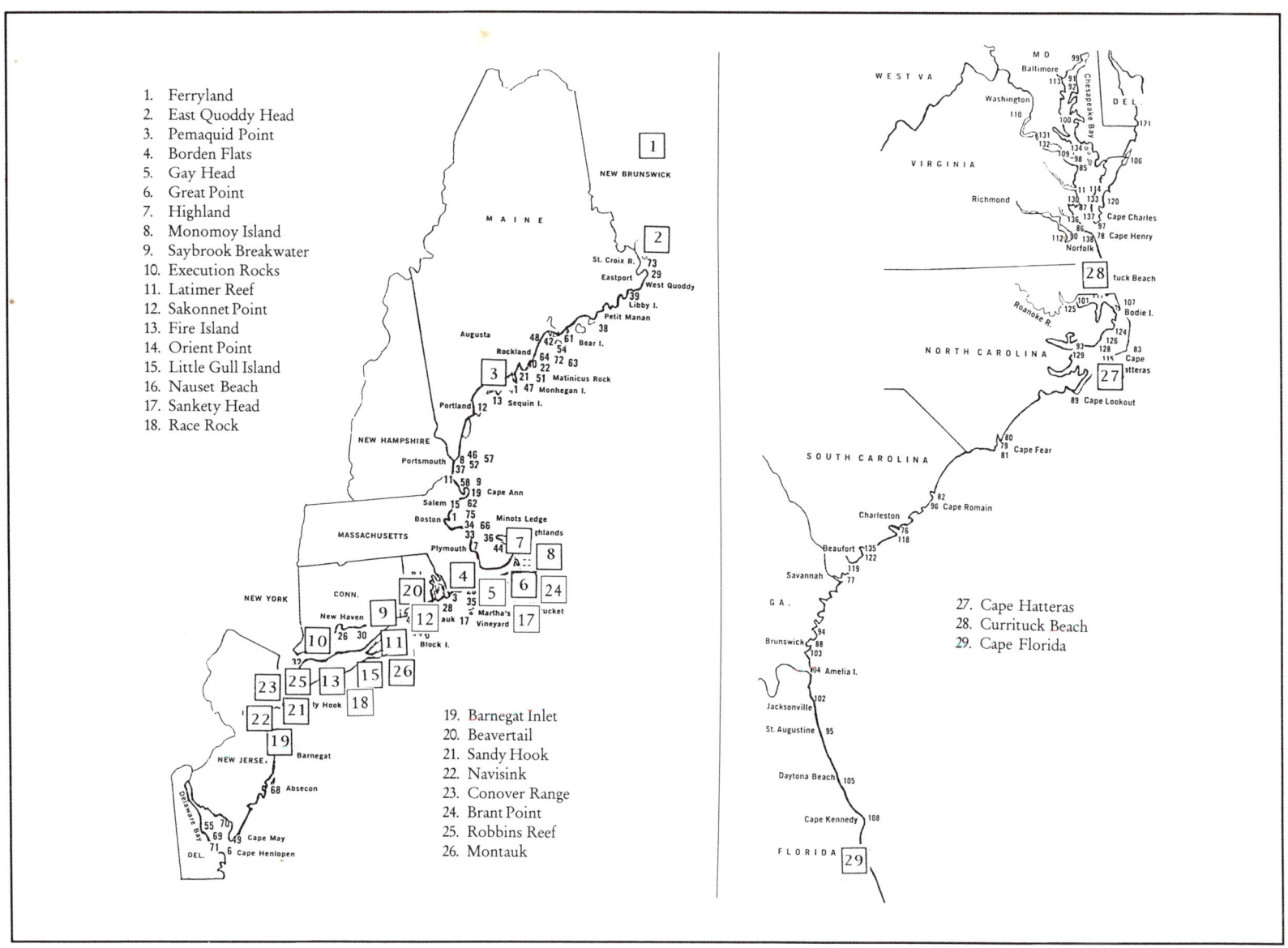

1. Ferryland
2. East Quoddy Head
3. Pemaquid Point
4. Borden Flats
5. Gay Head
6. Great Point
7. Highland
8. Monomoy Island
9. Saybrook Breakwater
10. Execution Rocks
11. Latimer Reef
12. Sakonnet Point
13. Fire Island
14. Orient Point
15. Little Gull Island
16. Nauset Beach
17. Sankety Head
18. Race Rock

19. Barnegat Inlet
20. Beavertail
21. Sandy Hook
22. Navisink
23. Conover Range
24. Brant Point
25. Robbins Reef
26. Montauk

27. Cape Hatteras
28. Currituck Beach
29. Cape Florida